ARCHPOETRY

ARCHPOETRY
URBAN ARCHITECTURE OF MALÉ
Finding Beauty and Serenity on a Concrete Island Garden

AHMAR MOHAMED • PHOTOGRAPHY BY ALES JUNGMANN

The Maldives
Location of the Maldives and its capital city, Malé

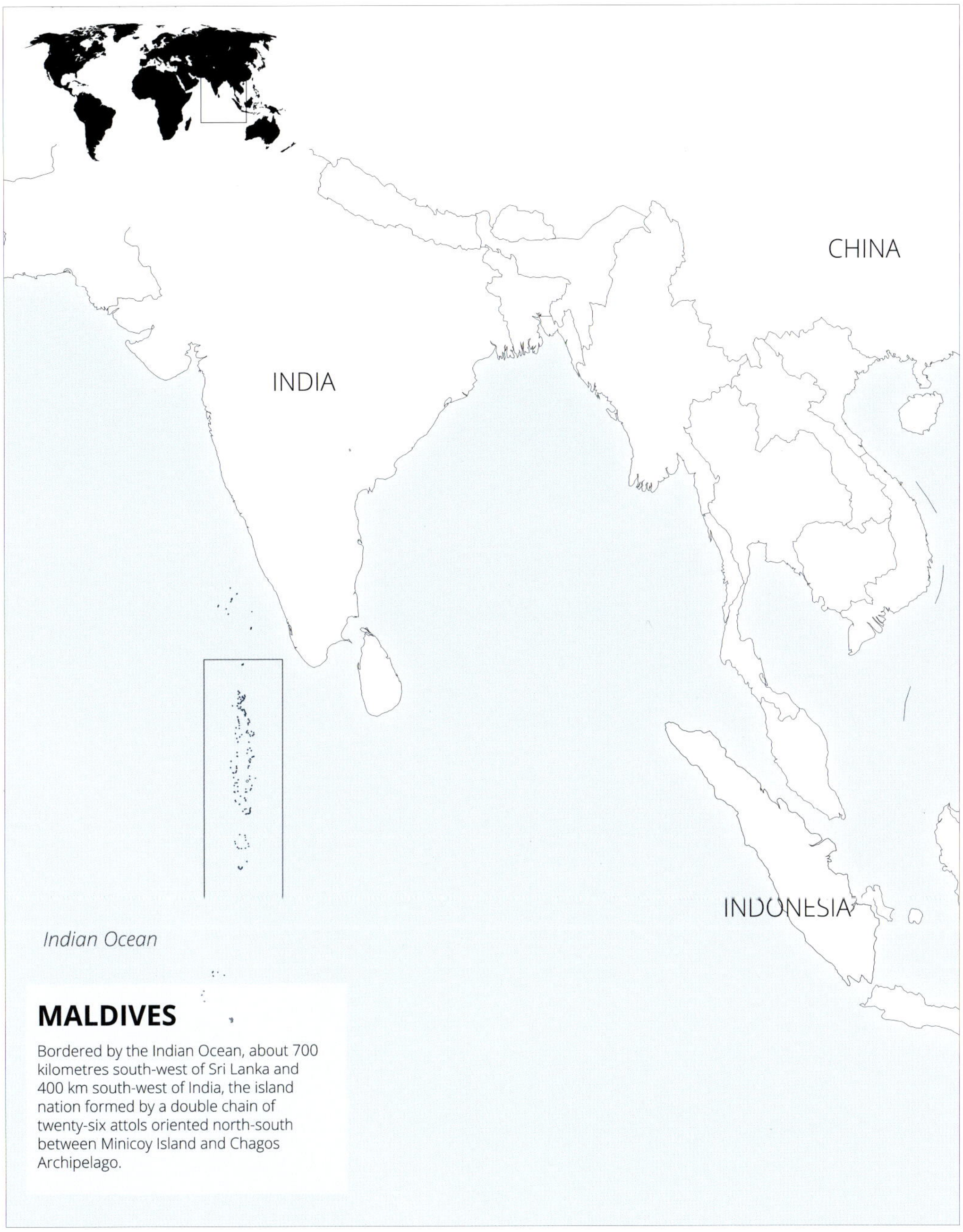

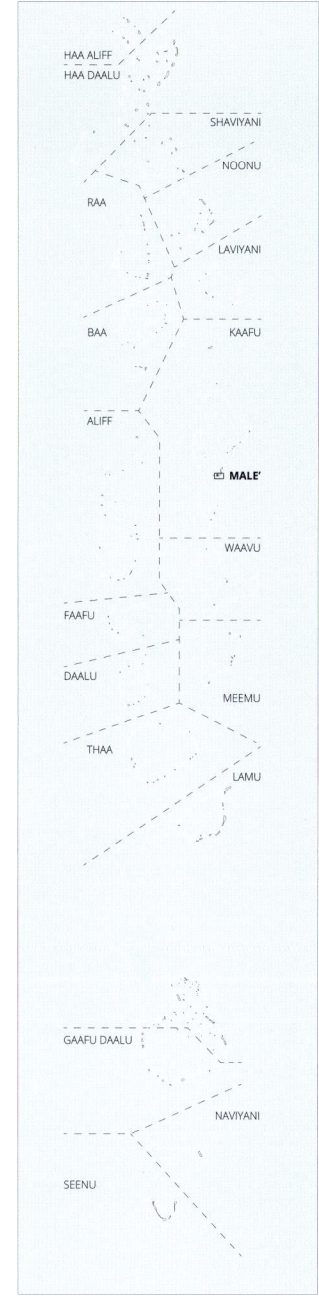

MALDIVES

Bordered by the Indian Ocean, about 700 kilometres south-west of Sri Lanka and 400 km south-west of India, the island nation formed by a double chain of twenty-six attols oriented north-south between Minicoy Island and Chagos Archipelago.

MALE'

The Maldives archipielago consists of 1,192 islands, but only 192 are inhabited. The capital of the Maldives is naturally located at the southern edge of North Malé Atoll, but it is not part of the Kaafu administrative division. It is the most populated city, with over 100,000 inhabitants on 5,798 km2

The Maldivian language is called Dhivehi, which is also the base word for "Maldivians" or the people of the Maldives.

It's an Indo-Aryan language based on Sanskrit, influenced by a number of languages including Arabic, French, Persian, Portuguese, Urdu and English. Major dialects are Maliku, Hadhunmathi, Mulku, Malé, Huvadhu and Addu. Malé dialect is the standard dialect.

The language is written in its own script from very ancient times.
The script is called Thaana. Thaana, like Hebrew and Arabic, is written from right to left.

Thaana consonants
Top row: Thaana letter; Middle rows: Nasir and New Latin letters; Bottom row: IPA symbols.

thaa	dhaalu	faafu	meemu	vaavu	alifu	kaafu	lhaviyani	baa	raa	noonu	rhaviyani	haa
th	dh	f	m	v	**vowel**	k	l	b	r	n	sh	h
th	dh	f	m	v	**vowel**	k	l	b	r	n	rh	h
[t]	[d]	[f]	[m]	[v]	Ø	[k]	[ɫ]	[b]	[r]	[n]	[ṣ]	[h]

zaviyani	sheenu	chaviyani	javiyani	paviyani	yaa	nyaviyani	taviyani	daviyani	seenu	dnaviyani	gaafu	laamu
z	sh'	ch	j	p	y	gn	t	d	s		g	l
z	sh	ch	j	p	y	ny	t	d	s	dn	g	l
[z]	[ʃ]	[c]	[ɟ]	[p]	[j]	[ɲ]	[ʈ]	[ɖ]	[s]	[ɳ]	[g]	[l]

Thaana vowel diacritics
Top row: Thaana letter; Middle rows: Nasir and New Latin letters; Bottom row: IPA symbols.

sukun	oaboafili	obofili	eybeyfili	ebefili	ooboofili	ubufili	eebeefili	ibifili	aabbaafili	abafili
?	oa	o	ey	e	oo	u	ee	i	aa	a
[ʔ]	[oː]	[o]	[eː]	[e]	[uː]	[u]	[iː]	[i]	[aː]	[a]

Letters used for translating Arabic words *(thiki jehi thaana)*
Top row: Thaana letter; Bottom row: the Arabic letters on which they are modelled.

waavu	qaafu	ghainu	ainu	zo	to	daadhu	saadhu	khaa	hhaa	thaalu	ttaa
w	q	gh	a'	z'	t'	l'	s'	kh	h'	dh'	th
w	q	gh	**vowel**	z	th	dz	s	kh	h	z	s
[w]	[q]	[ɣ]	[ʕ]	[zˤ]	[tˤ]	[dˤ]	[sˤ]	[x]	[ħ]	[ð]	[θ]

Introduction

Dhivehi Raaje is the authentic local word for the Maldives. The Maldives has always been a fascinating place for visitors who love the sunny, white sandy beaches, underwater beauty and the hospitality they get from islanders while they are on a resort.

What they don't often see is the life outside of the resort because the concept of tourism in the Maldives is a one-hotel-one-island concept. All that is worth seeing about Maldives and its people is just a step away from the resort life.

The concept of Dhivehin (local term for Maldivians) and how they thrive in the mist of the tourism income can only be seen by a visit to the capital city.

Malé – the capital city of the Maldives – is the living construction site of the country. The construction and design industry in the Maldives has largely been an automatic offshoot from the tourism industry – and we are still building every single day. Buildings play a huge role In the diversification of the dreams and aspirations of both the private and public lives of the Dhivehin (Maldivians).

When I first introduced the notion of the book, the idea of capturing the most important or valued building in city was on everyone's minds. However, we learned what matters to anyone is a matter of his or her own perception. And though we may not agree on what is most beautiful, our appreciation of beauty in general has led us to listen artfully.

And it's our hope that this book will ease minds and create a fluid exchange of ideas, in an effort to generate more concepts that are both simple and complex.

—Ahmar Mohamed, 2014

Life begins and ends with a seabreeze.

Eastern coastline of Malé.

Ariel view of the east coast of Malé, with the infamous "Artificial Beach", the capital's only beach.

Every day is a building day. No need for an alarm clock, the next door construction site makes the best alarm. We used to live in a happily wondered beauty.
We can all remember, but we don't see it anymore in this uniformity.
Loneliness, emptiness and separation are common in Malé. Before we could see where we grew our crops, but now there is a skyscraper. We are left to wonder if it is possible for us to stay and thrive.

Most of the buildings came about as means to earn an income in the island. The need for a better product grew as the need for the competition arises. The life of the building progresses with the life of the people it occupies. Our fast lives and desire to earn predominates the material life of the island.

The very standard form of shaping the skyline is square and cornered. Buildings become part of the other buildings. Most compliment each other, save a few. Unifying the simple needs of life.

The city wakes up at night from the dead sleep of the day. She is a real beauty at night. Charming. A walk at night tells you a different story. Buildings are more of them selves. They show their curves and edges. Yet, hardly anyone designed them with the nightlight in mind.

We are a product of the previous civilization. We make the next generation. If all generation comes from a previous product, all civilization is a mere understanding pattern followed by the previous generation. Generations and civilizations are a product infused in the past, present and future. Success needs to be our only future.

The Building of the Ministry of Foreign Affairs.

The view from east to west over the Maafanu district.

If you practice believing what you see and what you hear, it is not long before you train yourself to believe before you see or hear anything.
For islanders, far away news has always been fascinating, a story to be told as bedtime story to children. These were the first chanting calls.

The northeastern facade of the Supreme Court of the Maldives.

The island grew itself using the appropriated designs of other cultures, which have entangled the minds of Maldivians much more than they should have. Most of the structural details are ornaments -selfless beauty left to wander without function.

In Malé, confinement is a wonderland to be revisited over and over.

MEMORY
ހަނދުމަ

The coast guard's building and the Police Integrity Commission's building.

Its starts again. Immigrants aren't we all? Have we ever lived through our time? Have we not become who we tend to be, custodian of the islands?
We have not learned to be who we are. We never learned to live amongst ourselves. Will we ever lean to each other? Live in harmony with each other? Through all long moon nights. Our lives are part of your lives. Time is not for me to keep.

The president's office building.

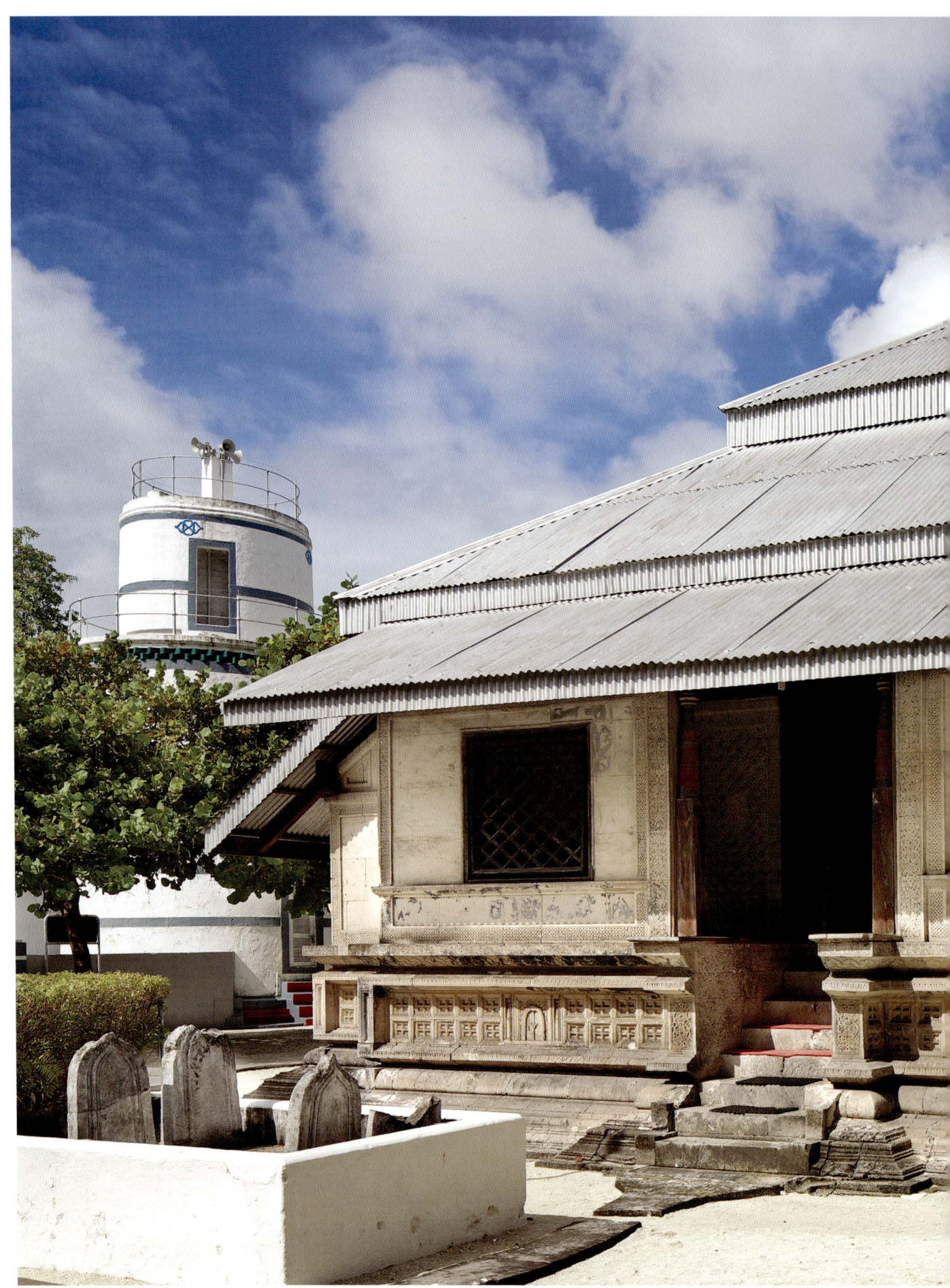
Hukuru Miskiy, translated as "Friday Mosque", one of the oldest mosques on the island of Malé.

Long before the islands become a well-known destination for keen sun worshipers, she mesmerized them when they were shipwrecked. She was wicked but pleasingly.

Faith, religion, people and culture. Faith is appreciating the liberty of trusting oneself outside the context of logical explanation. We did. Some of us forgot. People make mistakes, mistakes make people who they are. We were once still. Only structures are now. We have nothing left to remember but moving forward.

First built minaret of the Maldives in the historical area of the capital.

The November 3rd Memorial Square, with its monument on the right and the Grand Mosque in the background.

The official residence of the president of the Republic of Maldives.

People live in two dreams. Dreams of fantasy, dreams of forgetfulness.
Is all of our life in two states?
One above, one below. One out of mind, one sound-minded. People belong to places but often lack the appreciation of the place, what it means and how much impact it has on an average person's life. Nothing seems to motivate us, we are only dazed by the busy life.

The north entrance to the Grand Mosque, with minerat in the foreground.

The entrance to the University of the Maldives.

The faculty of Architecture at the University of the Maldives.

The former residence of the sultan during his reign, located in the Sultan's Park.

Every one loves their freedom of expression wherein a higher price is paid for ever-changing life. Long roofs and short windows. Doors that hardly open inside. Shelter for each other and shelter for the future.

The National Museum of the Maldives.

The structures and buildings are organic. They represent opportunities and functions, the desires of being, how it matters to our livelihood and how it impacts the community. It starts with an unconditional, emotional connection between built structures and natural surroundings. Reaching a point where art is the confined spaces we all live in. The love of colors, shapes and the free soul of the islanders have made some of the building we live in today into identical representations of the balance between busy life and the once free life we adored so much.

With experience we might learn, we might not. But if Almighty is willing, we will. The history a structure leaves is embedded in the minds of young ones, who might learn something out of it. In Malé, the oldest structures always dominate the oldest part of the island.

Life is just a delusional order of events. At least at sunset, a piece of chronological order unfolds expectedly. But most of the time, we operate somewhere between will and consent, tenderness and resentment past, heart felt memories and self-illusions; simultaneously united and disconnected by the events and what we believe about them.

Northwest gate of National Stadium.

We used to live in a happily wondered beauty.
We can all remember, but we don't see it anymore in this uniformity. Loneliness, emptiness and separation are common in Malé. Before we could see where we grew our crops, but now there is a high-rise. We are left to wonder if it is possible
for us to stay and thrive.

The facts are not what we think about. The choices we make and what comes out of them are not what we think about. Everything happening around us seemed normal in an exciting way. Our way is our way. Your way is your way. For us, the excitement of being in a dilemma is gone. The thought of sinking, the inevitable future of being washed away is now our way. It's our new normal.

Some days are better than others in a disproportionate way.
Days are just days when they are uncountable. But when
the inevitable ticking started, the survival instinct kicked in.
Surviving is methodology implied.

Nonsense is just another way of communicating.
At least on this island.

If we tend to expect more than what is really understood to the logical mind, the accepted consequences are something the logical mind does not understand. The logical mind likes straight lines.

Old buildings do not know that nothing lasts as long as wind and the waves. If you think it wont last, people should be more careful of what they choose to build. If we choose to build things without much thought and with improper technique, then the sea will choose our buildings' futures for us.

HOPE
ުއްމީދު

Limited space is a restriction to the open eye, but not the open mind.

Nightlife is never boring. The lampposts are no match for the light pollution from traffic. Buildings are lit up from outside in. Darkness is a luxury now. Nights and days are comparable. Who complains now? More light means more chances to work.

Most of the buildings are narrow long spaces, a product of a vertical division of the plot of land once owned proudly. Building titles are granted based on the divisions and its subdivision. Therefore, a fraction of a quarter of the land of the original plot becomes an area for a third generation.

Life is full of questions. Some are simple enough to not require an answer.
Some lead directly to answers and some to more questions. Some are answers in themselves. And some lead to more questions that are themselves the answers. In Malé, we can only try to find our way on the simplest terms.

Inward and outward. Who let us live selfishly? How does such a beautiful place have such a tenuous future? In Malé, we can see from our tightly packed apartments, our ornaments, our closeness, a way forward. An architecture of We. We shall not sit on sorrowful legs on roof tops waiting, but we shall live with each other and the wind and waves that bang on our door.

Office building with the Maldives Monetary Authority Building in the background.

People never intended to keep what is, leave what is not. What is expected out of them is the mirror effect of their own youth. In Malé, all structures breathe. It affects the life of people they host and shows a human relationship with Mother Nature.

The colors of the island's structures today are a reflection of the emptiness we once treasured so much. A feeling that was soon lost in the jumble of buildings that have replicated the colors a thousand times over on their facades. Visually, these colors appeal with a smile and an acknowledgment that they understand, and they are here too.

Life begins and ends with a seabreeze.

ORO Editions
Publishers of Architecture, Art, and Design
Publisher: Gordon Goff

www.oroeditions.com
info@oroeditions.com

www.pmo.mv
dropby@pmo.mv

Published by ORO Editions and PMO Pvt.
Copyright © ORO Editions and PMO Pvt. 2015

Author: Ahmar Mohamed
Photography by: Ales Jungmann
Edited by: Ryan Buresh
Graphic Design: Timea Török, Pablo Mandel
Production Assistance: Meghan Wright-Martin
Proofread by: Kristin Lacey

Texts are typeset in Bau OT

10 9 8 7 6 5 4 3 2 1 First Edition

Library of Congress data available upon request. World Rights: Available

ISBN : 978-1-941806-66-1

Color Separations and Printing: ORO Group Ltd.
Printed in China.

International Distribution: www.oroeditions.com/distribution

All rights reserved. No part of this book may be reproduced, stored in a retrieval system, or transmitted in any form or by any means,including electronic, mechanical, photocopying of microfilming, recording, or otherwise (except that copying permitted by Sections 107 and 108 of the U.S. Copyright Law and except by reviewers for the public press) without written permission from the publisher. You must not circulate this book in any other binding or cover and you must impose this same condition on any acquirer.

ORO Editions makes a continuous effort to minimize the overall carbon footprint of its publications. As part of this goal, ORO Editions, in association with Global ReLeaf, arranges to plant trees to replace those used in the manufacturing of the paper produced for its books. Global ReLeaf is an international campaign run by American Forests, one of the world's oldest nonprofit conservation organizations. Global ReLeaf is American Forests' education and action program that helps individuals, organizations, agencies, and corporations improve the local and global environment by planting and caring for trees.